EXPLORING
SCIENCE

ANIMAL CELLS

SMALLEST UNITS OF LIFE

BY DARLENE R. STILLE

Content Advisers: Michael Barresi, Ph.D., Assistant Professor,
Smith College, Northampton, Massachusetts
Debra Carlson, Ph.D., Faculty in Biology,
Normandale Community College, Bloomington, Minnesota

Science Adviser: Terrence E. Young Jr., M.Ed., M.L.S.,
Jefferson Parish (Louisiana) Public School System

Reading Adviser: Susan Kesselring, M.A., Literacy Educator,
Rosemount-Apple Valley-Eagan (Minnesota) School District

 COMPASS POINT BOOKS · MINNEAPOLIS, MINNESOTA

Compass Point Books • 3109 West 50th Street, #115 • Minneapolis, MN 55410

Visit Compass Point Books on the Internet at *www.compasspointbooks.com* or e-mail your request to *custserv@compasspointbooks.com*

Photographs ©: Ed Reschke/Peter Arnold, Inc., cover, 10; Photodisc, 4, 17; Flip Nicklin/Minden Pictures, 5; B. Parker/ Tom Stack & Associates, Inc., 6; Dr. David M. Phillips/Visuals Unlimited, 7, 21, 27; Digital Vision, 8, 14; Gary Meszaros/Visuals Unlimited, 9; Dr. D Spector/Peter Arnold, Inc., 12; Michael Abbey/Visuals Unlimited, 13; Liu Jin/AFP/Getty Images, 15; Dr. Gopal Murti/Visuals Unlimited, 16; Brand X Pictures, 18; Clouds Hill Imaging Ltd./Corbis, 19, 36; Creatas, 20; Dr. Gladden Willis/Visuals Unlimited, 24; Dr. John D. Cunningham/Visuals Unlimited, 25; Vincent/zefa/Corbis, 29; Dr. Dennis Kunkel/Visuals Unlimited, 30, 42; Dr. Richard Kessel & Dr. Gene Shih/Visuals Unlimited, 32; Norbert Schaefer/Corbis, 37; The Granger Collection, New York, 38; Inga Spence/Visuals Unlimited, 39; Dr. Brad Mogen/Visuals Unlimited, 40; UMW/Visuals Unlimited, 44; Lester V. Bergman/Corbis, 46.

Editor: Anthony Wacholtz
Designer/Page Production: The Design Lab
Photo Researcher: Marcie C. Spence
Illustrator: Eric Hoffmann

Art Director: Jaime Martens
Creative Director: Keith Griffin
Editorial Director: Carol Jones
Managing Editor: Catherine Neitge

Library of Congress Cataloging-in-Publication Data
Stille, Darlene R.
    Animal cells: the smallest units of life / by Darlene R. Stille.
        p. cm. — (Exploring science)
    Includes bibliographical references and index.
    ISBN 0-7565-1616-1 (hardcover)
    1. Cells—Juvenile literature. I. Title. II. Exploring science (Minneapolis, Minn.)
    QH582.5.S75 2006
    571.6'1—dc22   2005025059

    ISBN 0-7565-1761-3 (softcover)

(About the Author)

Darlene R. Stille is a science writer and author of more than 70 books for young people. When she was in high school, she fell in love with science. While attending the University of Illinois, she discovered that she also loved writing. She was fortunate enough to find a career as an editor and writer that allowed her to combine both of her interests. Darlene Stille now lives and writes in Michigan.

TABLE OF CONTENTS

CHAPTER ONE

From Ants to Elephants

ANTS HAVE STRONG MANDIBLES for gripping food. Butterflies have very delicate, colorful wings. Fish possess specialized gills for breathing. Hawks have keen eyes, allowing them to see tiny prey on the ground while they are high in the air. Humans, like many other animals, have spontaneously contracting muscle cells in their hearts.

All of the fascinating parts of these animals are made up of tiny cells. A cell is the smallest unit of life and provides the basic struc-

A butterfly's wings are an artistic display found in nature. Butterfly wings are made up of tiny cells.

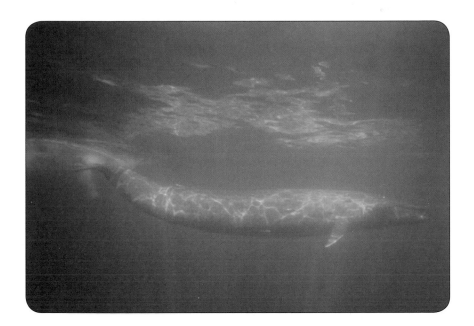

ture and function for every organism. Each animal cell is a living thing. It takes in food and gives off waste products. It grows and divides. Cells die, but they can be quickly replaced with new cells.

The bigger an organism is, the more cells it has. Some organisms, such as bacteria, are made up of only one cell. A human being is made up of 60 trillion to 100 trillion cells. The blue whale, the largest animal that ever lived on Earth, contains the most cells—it has approximately 1,000 times as many cells as a human being.

A blue whale, which contains the most cells of all animals, can eat up to 7,715 pounds (3,472 kilograms) of krill per day.

Amoebas

Scientists once thought certain one-celled organisms belonged to the animal kingdom. These one-celled organisms include amoebas. An amoeba can eat and give off waste products, reproduce by dividing, and move around by changing its shape and sticking out a projection called a pseudopod, or false foot.

Now scientists classify amoebas as neither animals nor plants. They are grouped as protozoans in a kingdom of one-celled organisms called Protista. Other one-celled organisms in the Protista kingdom include plasmodia, one-celled parasites that cause malaria.

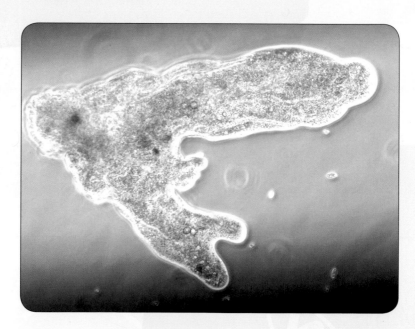

Like animal cells, an amoeba has a nucleus and cytoplasm inside its cell membrane.

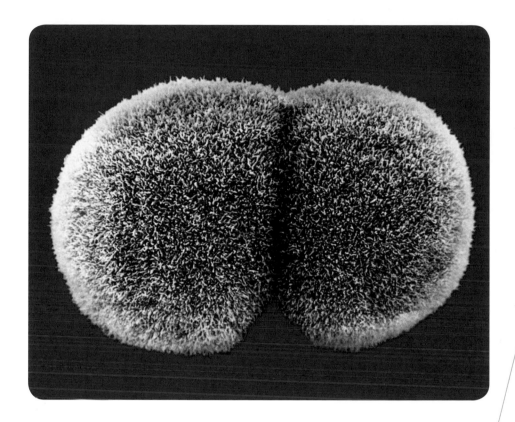

MANY CELLS FROM ONE CELL

No matter how many cells an organism grows up to have, all organisms begin as a single cell. The cell divides in half to form two cells, and the two cells divide again. The cells keep on dividing. Soon these cells are able to communicate with each other and form groups to take on different, specialized jobs. Some of these groups of cells become bone cells or skin cells. Others become muscle, blood, and nerve cells.

A mammal egg is undergoing a phase of cell division called cytokinesis. This phase occurs when there are two nuclei in the cell, ready to be separated into their own cells.

The very first groups of cells are nonspecialized, which means their function has not yet been assigned. As the cells develop into specific types, they combine to generate an embryo. As more and more cells form, the embryo grows until it reaches its full size, and a baby is born.

Even after a bear, dog, frog, or human being is grown up, its cells continue to divide. Some cells die, and new cells may take their place. By dividing when they have to and working together in just the right way, cells keep an organism healthy.

In order to remain healthy, a frog's cells will continue to divide after it has reached its maximum size.

What Animal Cells Look Like

MOST ANIMAL CELLS are so tiny that they can only be seen under a microscope. Some animal cells are fairly large. For example, frog eggs begin as cells, and some start out at 3 millimeters in diameter—the size of a small ant! Also, the white part you see when you crack open a chicken egg is actually an ovum, a female sex cell. The yellow yolk is a sac of food for the developing baby bird, and the hard shell around the egg is a coating of calcium. You don't need a microscope to see these cells!

Frog eggs are deposited in a large mass underwater. Before they start dividing, frog eggs are very large single animal cells.

Animal cells come in many different shapes. Muscle cells are long and thin. Nerve cells look like an octopus with long arms that reach out from a body in the center. Red blood cells are round and flat and look like discs. A cell's unique shape is specifically tailored to carry out a very special job.

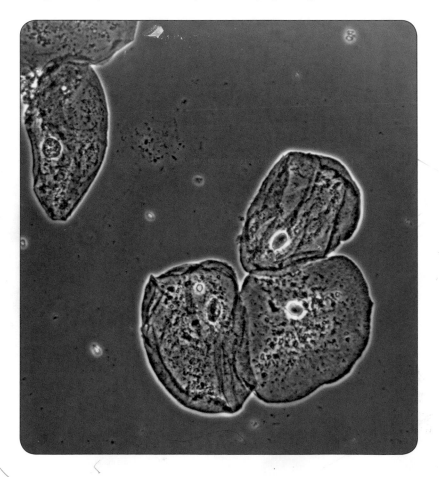

Human cheek cells magnified many times by a microscope

ANIMAL CELL

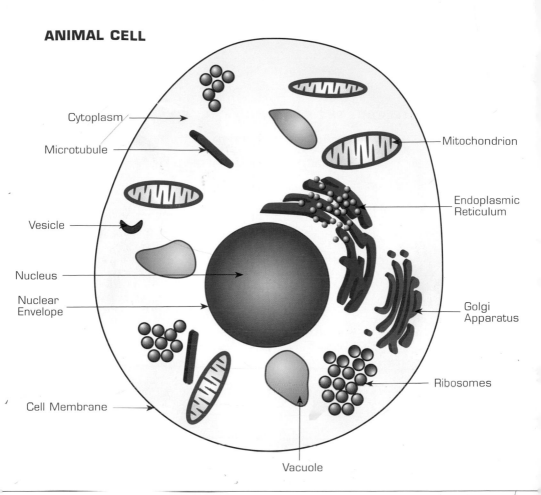

Cytoplasm

Microtubule

Mitochondrion

Vesicle

Endoplasmic Reticulum

Nucleus

Nuclear Envelope

Golgi Apparatus

Cell Membrane

Ribosomes

Vacuole

THE PARTS OF A CELL

No matter what an animal cell looks like, all animal cells are made of a substance called protoplasm. The protoplasm is inside a thin "baggie" called the cell membrane. Tiny openings in the cell membrane let chemical substances in or out. In most cells, the protoplasm has two main divisions called the nucleus and the cytoplasm.

NUCLEUS: THE COMMAND CENTER

Imagine that an animal cell is a restaurant. The nucleus is like the restaurant manager. Every part of the cell gets instructions from the nucleus, the command center of the cell. The nucleus is separated from the cytoplasm by a double "baggie" called the nuclear envelope. Genes in the nucleus "tell" cells what to do. The genes are made of a molecule called deoxyribonucleic acid (DNA) that carries a code for all of the cell's functions. The genes are located on tiny threadlike structures in the nucleus called chromosomes.

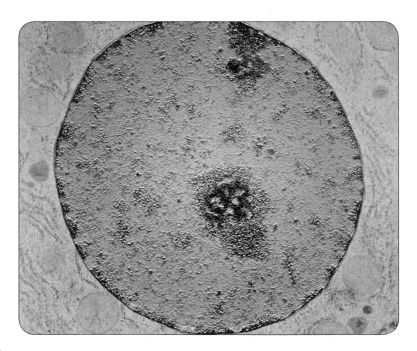

The nucleus in the liver cell of a mouse controls the actions performed within the cell.

Chromosomes in body cells of sexually reproducing organisms come in pairs. One chromosome in each pair comes from the organism's father. The other chromosome comes from the mother. Each species has a different number of chromosomes. For example, the body cells of a human being have 46 chromosomes, or 23 pairs. The body cells of a dog have 78 chromosomes, or 39 pairs. The body cells of a fruit fly have only eight chromosomes, or four pairs.

The chromosomes in each cell contain a complete set of genes for the whole organism. How can so many types of cells exist if they all have the same set of instructions (DNA) on the chromosomes? It is because each cell type is reading only a certain part of the instruction manual. It is through this process of gene regulation that a nerve cell looks and functions very differently from a muscle cell.

Chromosomes are found in the nucleus of the cell. A fruit fly's chromosomes look like numerous earthworms when magnified 400 times by a light microscope.

Chromosomes and Gender

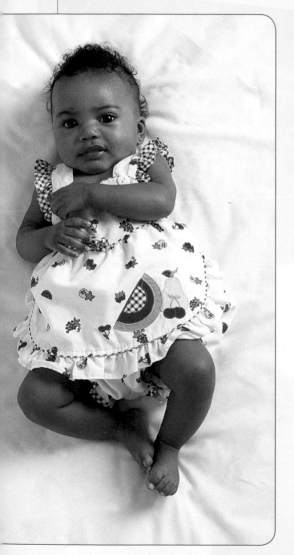

In human beings, chromosomes labeled as X and Y chromosomes determine a baby's gender. A fetus—a developing organism—with two X chromosomes will be a girl. A fetus with an X and a Y chromosome will be a boy. Eggs always have an X chromosome, but sperm may have either an X or a Y chromosome. When a Y-carrying sperm fertilizes an egg, the baby will be a boy (XY). When an X-carrying sperm fertilizes an egg, then the baby will be a girl (XX).

Baby girls are born when the Y chromosome is absent.

CYTOPLASM: THE WORK CENTER

The cytoplasm houses all the appropriate equipment to carry out the cell's functions. The cytoplasm is like a restaurant's kitchen, not because food is prepared there, but because it is where the work of the cell gets done.

Structures in the cytoplasm called organelles make sure the cell functions as it should. Most animal cells have three main organelles: the endoplasmic reticulum, the Golgi apparatus, and the mitochondria. Many ribosomes are attached to the outside of the endoplasmic reticulum. Ribosomes are the kitchen counters of the cell. They help assemble proteins by linking together chemical units called amino acids. The resulting proteins are folded into the Golgi apparatus and packaged into vesicles, which are like small pouches. Like servers at a restaurant carrying food to the customers, transport units called microtubules carry these vesicles around the cell.

The cytoplasm is the work center and functions like the kitchen in a restaurant.

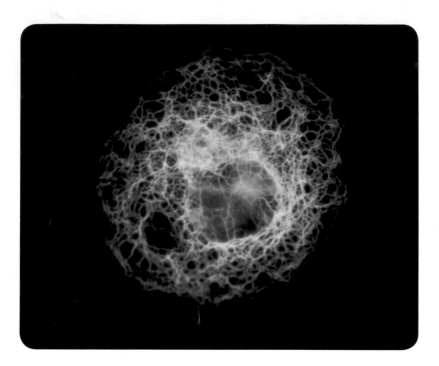

THE CYTOSKELETON

A cell, of course, does not have bone. However, rodlike protein fibers form what scientists call the cytoskeleton of a cell. The cytoskeleton is what gives various cells their shapes. By extending parts of the cytoskeleton, some cells can move in the spaces between cells and "crawl" over other cells.

DID YOU KNOW?

The cytoskeleton acts as both a muscle and a skeleton.

The cytoskeleton is responsible for splitting the cell membrane during cytokinesis and moving the chromosomes during cell division.

HOW DO CELLS GET THEIR ENERGY?

After playing a long game of soccer or baseball, our bodies are
tired and need food and water. Just as our bodies get hungry
for energy, so do our cells. In fact, the hunger of individual
cells is what creates the feeling of hunger that we experience.
All of this activity calls for plenty of energy.

Energy comes from the mitochondria, the powerhouses
of the cell. The mitochondria get their fuel from the food we
eat. First, the food must be broken down into a form that the
cells can use.

A baseball player needs plenty of energy, which comes from the food he eats.

A chicken dinner, a piece of fruit, and a hamburger on a bun are broken down by the body into smaller and smaller parts. This breaking down is called digestion. The process begins in the mouth, where food gets chewed and mixed with saliva. The food goes to the stomach, where powerful acids further break the fruit and bun into carbohydrates. Chicken and beef get broken down into proteins and fats.

From the stomach, food goes to the intestine, where the job of digestion gets finished. There the protein is broken into amino acids. The fat becomes fatty acids, and the carbohydrates become simple sugars. These simple food substances go through the intestinal wall and into the bloodstream. The blood carries these substances to cells everywhere in the body.

The cell membrane lets the food substances into the cell. The mitochondria then convert the chemical energy in the food into a chemical called adenosine triphosphate (ATP), which provides the energy that the cell needs to perform all of its functions.

The food we eat is broken down into a form of energy that our bodies can use.

Differences Between Animal and Plant Cells

Several features make animal cells different from plant cells. Animal cells have flexible cell membranes that allow those cells to take on different shapes. Plant cells have rigid cell walls that make most of those cells square- or rectangular-shaped.

Some animal cells have small sacs called vacuoles, but all plant cells have a large central vacuole. When the vacuole is full of water, the flowers and leaves look full. When there is little or no water in the vacuole, plants droop and look wilted.

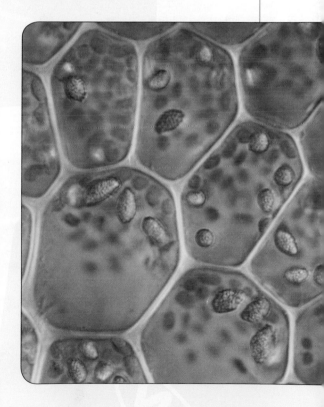

In addition, green plant cells make a substance called chlorophyll. Plants use chlorophyll, along with carbon dioxide gas from the air and energy from the sun, to make their own food. Animal cells do not make chlorophyll. Animal cells get their energy from the food that the animal eats.

Although similar in some ways, plant cells have different shapes and functions than animal cells.

The Jobs That Animal Cells Do

THE BODY OF AN ORGANISM has many different kinds of cells. Each kind of cell has a special job to do. Muscle cells are responsible for moving the arms and legs of humans, the tails of alligators, and the trunks of elephants. Nerve cells send messages to, and receive messages from, cells in muscles, skin, eyes, and other sense organs. There are cells that form organs, such as the liver, lungs, or stomach. Still other cells patrol the body like watchdogs on the alert for germs or other foreign invaders. To do their jobs, the different kinds of cells use their parts differently.

The powerful muscles in an alligator's tail allow it to move quickly in the water and defend itself against other animals.

TALENTED BLOOD CELLS

There are two kinds of blood cells—red and white—that do very different work. Red blood cells carry oxygen from the lungs to all the cells of the body. Similarly, they carry carbon dioxide away from the cells and to the lungs for exhaling. White blood cells make up the body's disease-fighting immune system.

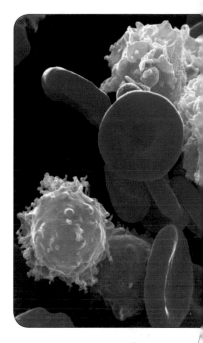

A mature red blood cell is the only kind of cell that lacks a nucleus. A young red blood cell has a nucleus, but the nucleus disappears when the cell matures. A mature red blood cell is made mainly of the protein hemoglobin. Hemoglobin plays an important role in breathing. Hemoglobin picks up oxygen from the lungs and carries it through blood vessels to the cells. Then the hemoglobin picks up some of the carbon dioxide gas, a waste product, and carries it to the lungs.

To flow easily through the blood vessels, red blood cells are round, smooth, and shaped like a flattened disk. They have a very flexible cell membrane that lets them squeeze through the narrowest blood vessels called capillaries. You would have to stack 100 red blood cells on top of each other just to equal the thickness of a dime!

Although they are both vital to an animal's well-being, red and white blood cells carry out different functions.

DID YOU KNOW?

People who live at high altitudes have more red blood cells than people who live at sea level. The higher you go, the less oxygen there is in the air. Because they have more red blood cells to pick up oxygen, the body cells of people living at high altitudes can get all the oxygen they need to be healthy.

White blood cells may reside in various organs through-out the body. Otherwise they patrol through the bloodstream. These blood cells have a cell membrane that forms many spikelike projections. These spikes help white cells find for-eign invaders. Several special kinds of white blood cells work together to fight infections. Some white blood cells send out an alarm when their spikes detect invaders. Other white blood cells contain many organelles that give off a protein that is deadly to germs. These white blood cells surround and kill germs and diseased cells.

MUSCLE CELLS: MOVERS AND SHAKERS

Body parts move, stomachs rumble, and hearts beat because of muscle cells. There are three types of muscle cells—skeletal, smooth, and cardiac muscle.

Skeletal muscles—the muscles that connect bones and move arms and legs—are made of long, thin cells. When we

TYPES OF MUSCLE

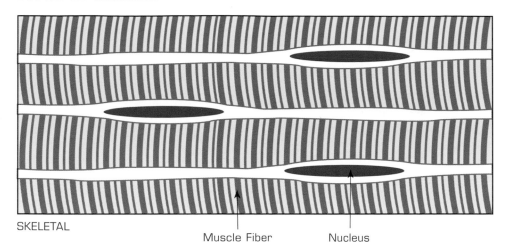

SKELETAL

Muscle Fiber   Nucleus

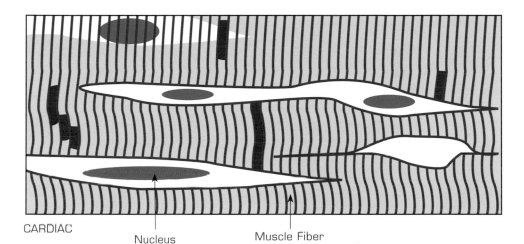

CARDIAC   Nucleus   Muscle Fiber

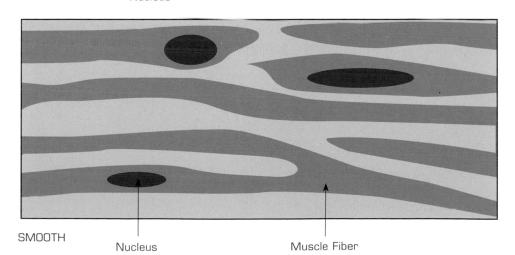

SMOOTH   Nucleus   Muscle Fiber

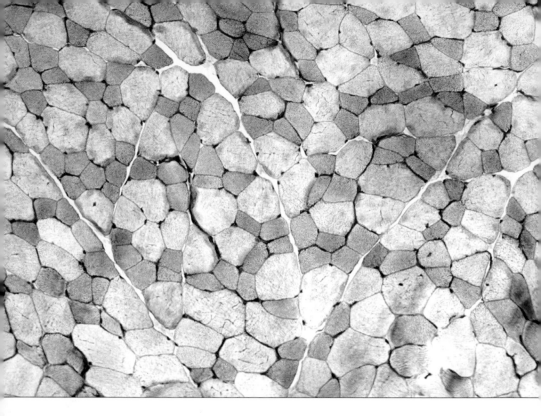

need to move, signals from our brain travel down a nerve network to a motor neuron, a nerve cell that sends messages from the nervous system to muscles and other tissues. There the signal is transferred to skeletal muscle, and the muscle shortens, or contracts. Thus, our arm or leg moves!

Because of their shape, muscle cells are also called muscle fibers. Under a microscope, skeletal muscle cells look like they have light and dark bands. The bands are really strands of two proteins called myosin and actin. These protein strands move past each other and cause the muscle to contract. Each skeletal muscle cell has more than one nucleus because the fibers form when existing immature cells in a fetus join to form one large cell. Muscle cells also have hundreds of mitochondria to

Skeletal muscles must be triggered by the nervous system.

convert all the energy that muscles need to work.

Smooth muscle makes up the walls of an animal's blood vessels, intestines, stomach, and other organs. Smooth muscle cells are smaller than skeletal muscle cells and have only one nucleus. Smooth muscle cells work involuntarily, which means they move without our having to think about them. The ability of smooth muscle cells to "think" on their own is vitally important for our circulatory system to work.

Cardiac muscle cells make up the tissue of our hearts.

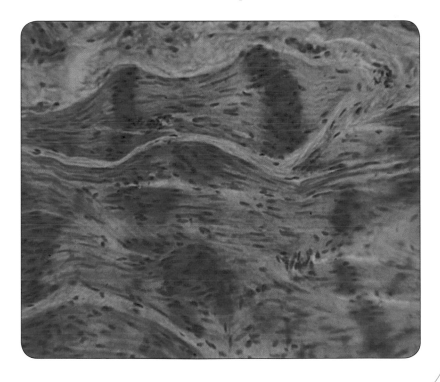

Smooth muscles look much different from skeletal and cardiac muscles.

Like smooth muscle cells, cardiac muscle cells have only one nucleus and work automatically to make the heart beat and to push blood through the body. Like skeletal muscle cells, cardiac muscle cells have bands.

NERVE CELLS: GREAT COMMUNICATORS

Nerve cells, or neurons, are designed to carry messages. A nerve cell has a center, or cell body, that processes signals coming into and going out of the cell. Several long fibers stretch out like arms from the cell body toward other nerves. These fibers are called axons and dendrites. Many nerve cells have one axon and several dendrites. The axon carries mes-

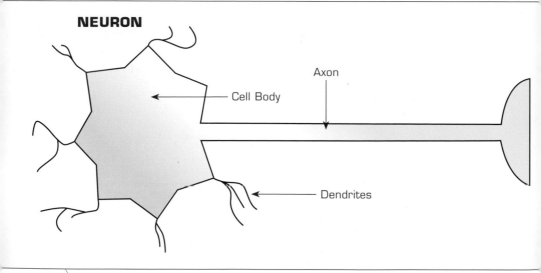

NEURON

Cell Body

Axon

Dendrites

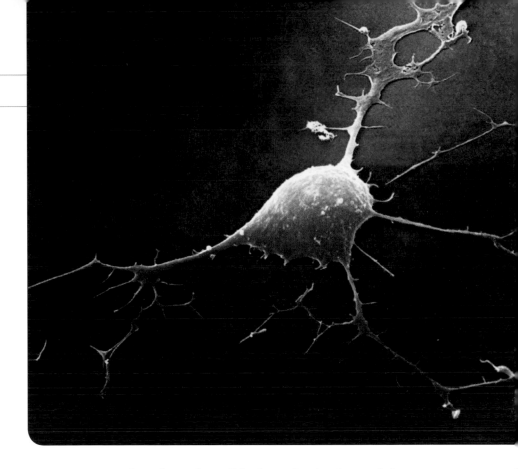

sages, or impulses, from the cell body to the dendrites of the next neuron. The dendrites pass the signal along to the cell body, which sends it on through the axon. Many neurons bundle together to form a large network that carries messages to and from the brain.

Special nerve cells carry out special tasks. Sensory neurons pick up messages about the outside world, such as tastes, textures, sights, smells, and sounds. The nerve network sends these messages from the sensory neurons to the brain. The brain contains billions of nerve cells that process the information and decide what to do. Brain neurons send instructions to

The motor neuron of a human being receives messages from the brain.

other nerve cells called motor neurons. Motor neurons carry messages to glands and skeletal, smooth, and cardiac muscles.

For example, sensory neurons in the eye send a message that the brain interprets as a piece of pie. Nerve cells in the brain send out a series of messages to motor neurons in the spinal cord, which in turn sends messages to axons that are connected to muscle cells in the arm and hand. These messages tell the hand to pick up a fork and use it to deliver a portion of the pie to the mouth.

SKIN CELLS: THE BODY'S PROTECTION

Skin cells protect other cells inside an organism's body. In humans, the top part of the skin, the epidermis, is a thin sheet that covers most of the body. The epidermis is made up of several layers of skin cells, with each layer having a different job to do.

Skin cells in the outer layer, or horny layer, are dead. These cells make the skin waterproof because they contain a tough protein called keratin. Dead skin cells wash off when we take a bath or shower. They also fall off and contribute to the dust in our homes.

Skin cells in the middle layers contain substances that make keratin. The bottom layer of cells in the epidermis is called the basal layer. The main job of basal cells is to make

new skin cells to replace the ones that die. Some skin cells stay in the basal layer and make a protein called melanin, which protects against harmful rays from the sun. Other basal cells move upward and finally become cells of the horny layer.

Our skin produces melanin, which causes our skin to darken after long periods of time outside.

CHAPTER FOUR

How Cells Divide and Multiply

CELLS DO NOT LIVE FOREVER. Nerve cells live the longest, sometimes more than 100 years! Skin cells, on the other hand, live for only a few weeks. When cells die, they must be replaced to keep the organism healthy. Cells replace lost cells by dividing. One cell divides to create two new cells.

An organism has two basic kinds of cells—body cells and sex cells. Body cells are also called somatic cells. These cells make up all the tissues of the body, from nerves and skin to organs and blood. Each somatic cell contains pairs of chromosomes.

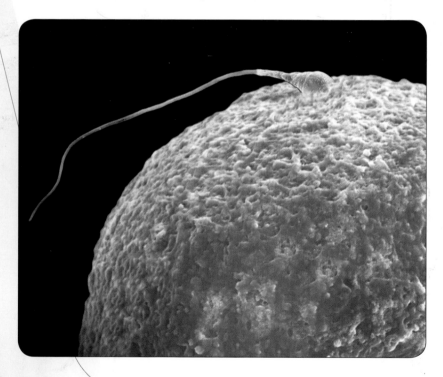

A sperm penetrates an egg during sexual reproduction.

DID YOU KNOW?

Not all animals need sex cells to reproduce. For example, a worm called a planarian reproduces asexually. Its body divides into two sections, and these sections become fully functional worms. This process is called regeneration.

Sex cells—called germ cells or gametes—unite in sexual reproduction to make new organisms. Eggs are female germ cells, and sperm are male germ cells. Each germ cell carries only half the number of chromosomes that somatic cells carry. This way, when a male and female germ cell come together, the correct number of chromosomes is achieved.

Body cells and sex cells replicate in different ways. Body cells divide in a process called mitosis, while sex cells are made through meiosis.

MITOSIS: A BODY CELL DIVIDES

Cell division is a complicated process that allows organisms to generate new cells for growth and replace dead or diseased cells for health maintenance. The goal of mitosis is to produce two identical body cells with the same genes on the same pairs of chromosomes.

Before mitosis can begin, chromosomes in the nucleus make copies of themselves. The copies are called sister chroma-

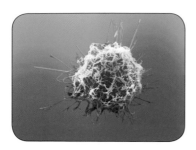

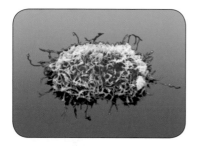

tids. Each pair of sister chromatids is joined in the middle by a structure called a centromere, making the shape of an X. Once this joining happens, mitosis can begin. There are four stages of mitosis: prophase, metaphase, anaphase, and telophase.

During the first stage, prophase, protein fibers make a structure in the center of the nucleus called a spindle. At the opposite ends of the spindle, structures called centrosomes move to opposite ends. In the second stage, metaphase, the sister chromatids line up on opposite sides of the middle, of the spindle. In the third stage, anaphase, sister chromatids divide, move down the spindle toward opposite ends, and become new chromosomes. During the final stage, telophase, the spindle disassembles and nuclear membranes form around each new set of chromosomes. The cytoplasm pinches together between the two nuclei, and two new cells, called daughter cells, form.

A cell goes through the four stages of mitosis.

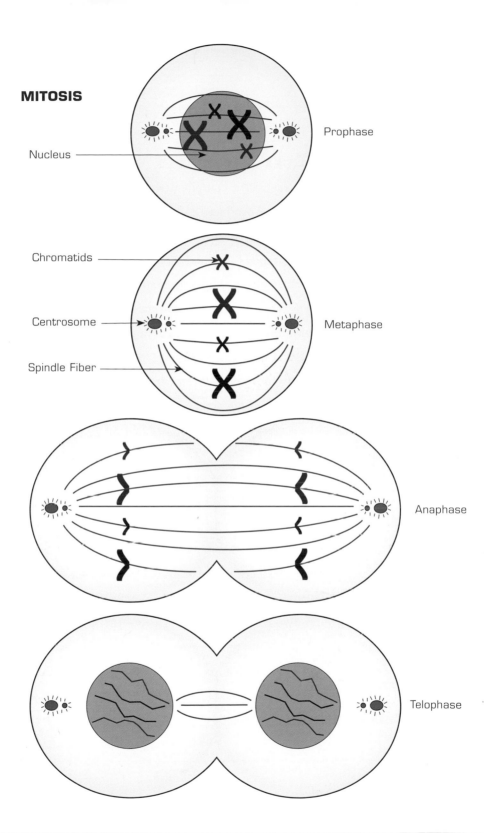

MITOSIS

Prophase

Nucleus

Chromatids

Centrosome

Metaphase

Spindle Fiber

Anaphase

Telophase

MEIOSIS: A SEX CELL DIVIDES

Like mitosis, meiosis is a complicated process. However, the goal of meiosis is to produce sex cells with only one set of chromosomes.

Sex cells are needed for sexual reproduction. A child inherits one set of chromosomes from the father and one set from the mother. The father's chromosomes are contained in sperm, and the mother's chromosomes are contained in the egg. When the sperm enters and fertilizes the egg, the cell then has two pairs of each chromosome—one set from the father and one set from the mother. This single cell then divides again and again by mitosis. The newly formed cells group and specialize to become a new organism.

Eggs are made by meiosis in female sex organs called ovaries. Sperm are made in male sex organs called testes. Cells in these organs have two sets of chromosomes, one set from the organism's mother and one from the father. They divide to make new sex cells by meiosis. As in mitosis, the chromosomes make copies of themselves before meiosis begins.

There are two parts to meiosis. During the first part, the chromosomes form into pairs, each chromosome consisting of two sister chromatids. The pairs of chromosomes line up in the middle and then move to opposite ends. The cytoplasm divides, forming two daughter cells. Each cell has half the

MEIOSIS

Chromatids

Spindle Fiber

Centrosome

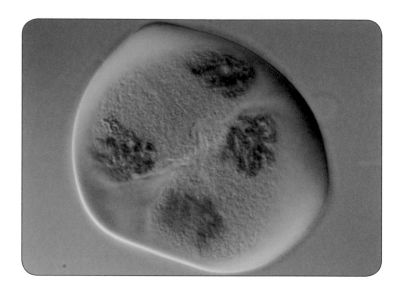

number of chromosomes as the original cell, and each chromosome still consists of two sister chromatids. The nucleus and the cytoplasm divide, forming two cells containing the sister chromatids. One sister chromatid is from the individual's mother, and the other is from the father.

The second part of meiosis is similar to mitosis. The chromosomes, each consisting of two sister chromatids, line up at the middle in each of the two cells. The sister chromatids of the chromosomes then split apart and move to opposite ends of the cell. After the cytoplasm divides, there are four daughter cells, each containing one set of chromosomes. These cells will become the sex cells.

A cell divides twice during meiosis, creating four daughter cells.

Genetic Variation

Have you ever wondered why, even though they have similarities, members of a family look so different from one another? One reason is that the chromosomes get shuffled around during meiosis. When a sex cell divides to form four daughter cells, some single chromosomes in a cell will be from the individual's father and some from the mother. In addition, when the chromosomes are close together during meiosis, parts of one chromosome can switch places with the same parts on another chromosome. This switch is called crossing over.

Although members of a family tend to look alike, they often have defining features that set them apart from the rest of the family.

CHAPTER FIVE

Studying Animal Cells

THE FIRST PERSON TO SEE A CELL was an English scientist named Robert Hooke. In 1665, while looking at a slice of cork (dead plant cells) under a microscope, he saw what looked like walls around many holes. He called the walls and the holes inside *cellulae*, which is Latin for "little rooms." Early scientists thought that cells were interesting, but they had no idea what cells really were.

Almost two centuries later, in the 1830s, German scientists Matthias Schleiden and Theodor Schwann independently came up with the idea that cells are the building blocks of all organisms. With more powerful microscopes invented in the late 1800s, scientists were able to see the organelles and watch how cells divide.

Besides discovering cells, Robert Hooke also invented many things, including the balance wheel in a watch.

HOW SCIENTISTS STUDY CELLS

The main tool for studying animal cells is the microscope. Microscopes let scientists see all but the tiniest details by magnifying the cells. Ordinary microscopes, called optical microscopes, can make a cell look 2,000 times bigger than it is. Powerful electron microscopes can magnify a cell up to 200,000 times.

With the invention of scanning electron microscopes, scientists can now examine cells in much more detail.

Cells must be prepared so they can be seen under a microscope. Often researchers use a centrifuge, a machine that can separate solids, such as cells, from liquids. Scientists separate blood cells from other parts of the blood with a centrifuge. Sometimes they grind up tissue and put it in a centrifuge to separate out cells.

First they put blood or a tissue sample in a test tube and

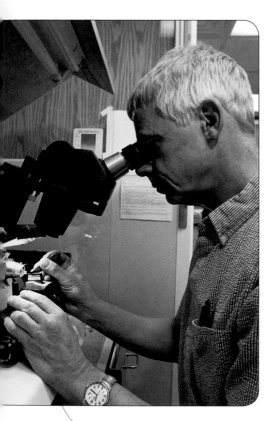

set the test tube into a centrifuge. The centrifuge has a wheel that whirls rapidly, causing heavier cells to settle out of the liquid and fall to the bottom of the test tube. Next the cells must be placed on a slide for viewing under a microscope. The layer of cells must be thin enough so that light from an optical microscope can pass through them. A thin layer of cells or a thin slice of tissue containing the cells can be placed on the slide.

Scientists can also use an instrument called a microtome to cut tissue samples that have

Using a microtome, scientists can reduce the size of the tissue sample so it can be easily viewed under a microscope.

been frozen or dried out. The sharp knife in a microtome cuts slices that are 1/2,500 inch (0.01 millimeter) thick. A special microtome cuts even thinner slices—1/1,300,000 inch (0.02 micrometer) thick—thin enough for the electron beam of an electron microscope to go through.

Once the layer of cells is thin enough, one other problem must be overcome. The parts of most cells are transparent. In order to make the different parts stand out, scientists stain the cells with dyes. Cells stained and mounted on a microscope slide are ready to be studied.

CELLS AND DISEASE

Sometimes problems with body cells lead to disease. Cells that divide inappropriately—at the wrong place and at the wrong time—can cause a disease called cancer. Rapidly dividing cells can form lumps called tumors. Cells from cancerous tumors can travel through the body, forming new tumors in the lungs, liver, skin, and other organs.

Other diseases come from cells that do not work properly. For example, a disease called sickle cell anemia is caused by red blood cells that do not have the correct shape to flow smoothly through blood vessels.

Sometimes viruses get inside cells and cause disease. Some viruses cause mild diseases such as colds or the flu, while

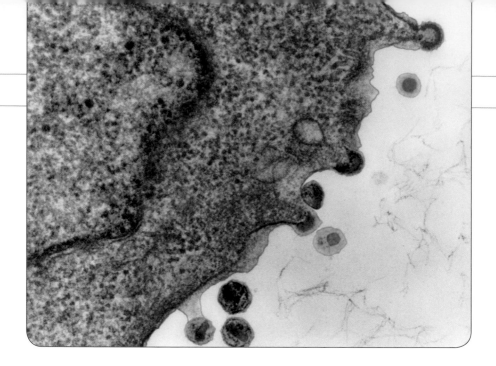

other viruses attack specific types of cells and can be more severe. For example, human immunodeficiency virus (HIV) attacks the cells of the immune system and prevents the body from defending itself against other viruses.

WHY STUDY CELLS?

Scientists study cells for many reasons. They want to find out how and why cells change, function, communicate, and interact with other cells, as well as why cells die. Doctors and medical scientists study cells to look for signs of illness or disease. They count the number of red and white cells in the blood. They look for abnormal cells that could lead to cancer or other diseases. Learning new things about animal cells could help scientists find cures and treatments for many different medical conditions.

The human immunodeficiency virus attacks a cell.

Much modern scientific research centers on the cell nucleus and the genes that it contains. Scientists want to know if they can use knowledge about genes to cure illnesses such as sickle cell anemia and cystic fibrosis that are caused by defects in cells. Medical researchers believe that studying cells will lead to cures for diseases that were once thought to be hopeless.

Researchers have learned a lot about animal cells. They have learned how and why cells divide and multiply. They have learned about the jobs that each kind of cell does. There are still many mysteries about cells waiting to be solved. Why do cells suddenly "go bad" and cause cancer? How can sick cells be fixed when a virus invades them and causes colds, flu, or AIDS? One of the greatest mysteries about cells, however, is how do all the different kinds of cells that make up an organism—blood, nerve, bone, skin, and muscle cells—come from just a single cell?

DID YOU KNOW?

Scientists called developmental biologists study how single cells divide, multiply, and differentiate, or become all the various kinds of cells that make up an animal's body.

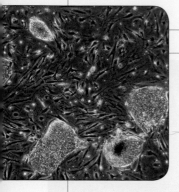

Stem Cells

Stem cells are unique because their "job" has not yet been determined. They have not specialized into a muscle, skin, blood, or other type of cell.

Any kind of cell in the body can develop from an embryonic stem cell—the first cells in a newly created organism. This means that the embryo is totipotent—its stem cells can give rise to any cell in an organism. The fertilized egg divides to form a hollow ball of cells called a blastocyst in higher organisms, like humans, or a blastula in lower organisms. The blastocyst and blastula are made up of stem cells. Blood, bone, skin, nerve, muscle, and all other kinds of cells can form from these stem cells.

Scientists have learned how to grow other cells from human embryonic stem cells in laboratories. They believe they can use these stem cells to cure many otherwise incurable diseases, such as Parkinson's disease, Alzheimer's disease, and diabetes.

People argue about the use of stem cells in research. Some people believe it is wrong because human embryos may be destroyed. Other people say that the embryos should be used because of the potential to help people who are sick or disabled. Today stem cell research is a highly debated topic in Congress as well.

Stem cell research is an exciting but controversial topic.

amino acids—building blocks of proteins

ATP (adenosine triphosphate)—chemical that cells use for energy

axon—arm of a nerve cell that sends out signals

body cell—also called somatic cell; most of the cells in the body containing two sets of chromosomes.

chromatid—a copy of a chromosome; chromatids occur in pairs after DNA replication, prior to mitosis or meiosis

chromosome—threadlike structure that carries genes

cytoplasm—fluid part of the cell where all cell functions are carried out

dendrite—arm of a nerve cell that receives signals

DNA (deoxyribonucleic acid)—chemical of which genes are made

gene—basic unit of heredity and code for functions of a cell

meiosis—cell division that produces eggs and sperm

microscope—an instrument used for magnification

mitochondria—organelles that convert energy from one chemical form to another

mitosis—division of body cells

neuron—nerve cell

nucleus—command center of the cell

protoplasm—material inside a cell that contains two main divisions, the nucleus and cytoplasm

protein—one of the four types of large molecules (along with lipids, carbohydrates, and nucleic acids) that make up cells

ribosome—structure that helps assemble proteins

RNA (ribonucleic acid)—a copy of DNA used to assemble proteins

sex cell—egg or sperm, containing only one set of chromosomes

stem cell—type of cell that can give rise to any other kind of cell

▶ Cells form tissues, and tissues form organs. Animal cells are bound together by proteins to form tissues and organs.

▶ Genes are made of a chemical called DNA. It provides codes for proteins. A similar chemical called RNA carries DNA instructions through the nuclear membrane and into the cytoplasm, where proteins get assembled.

▶ The same kind of hardened skins that form the outer layer of the epidermis form finger and toe nails in humans. These hardened skin cells form claws and talons on birds and horns and hoofs on other animals.

▶ The cell membrane is semipermeable. This means that it lets certain substances pass into and out of the cell. It blocks out other substances.

▶ When body cells are between divisions, chromatin—the material that chromosomes are made of—is hard to see under a microscope. When a cell begins to divide, the chromosomes get shorter and thicker. They can then be seen under a microscope.

▶ Individuals created from the mother's and father's sex cells inherit chromosomes passed on from their grandparents.

▶ New red blood cells come from red bone marrow, a soft material at the center of some bones in adults. Human bone marrow makes millions of blood cells every second. Red cells mature and go right to the blood stream. Some white cells go to other organs called the lymph nodes, thymus, or spleen, where they mature.

▶ The nucleolus inside the nucleus makes ribosomes. Ribosomes go to the cytoplasm, where they make all the proteins that the cell needs.

▶ The cell membrane is also called the plasma membrane. It is made up mainly of lipids (fats), carbohydrates, and proteins.

Besides producing red blood cells, bone marrow houses two types of stem cells.

At the Library

DuPrau, Jeanne. *Cells.* San Diego: Kidhaven Press, 2002.
George, Michael. *Cells: Building Blocks of Life.* Mankato, Minnesota: Creative Education, 2003.
Gillie, Oliver. *Sickle Cell Disease.* Chicago: Heinemann Library, 2004.
Snedden, Robert. *Animals: Multicelled Life.* Oxford: Heinemann Library, 2002.

On the Web

For more information on **Animal Cells,** use FactHound to track down Web sites related to this book.
1. Go to *www.facthound.com*
2. Type in a search word related to this book or this book ID: **0756516161**
3. Click on the *Fetch It* button.
FactHound will find the best Web sites for you.

On the Road

Animal Biology Exhibit
The Field Museum
1400 S. Lake Shore Drive
Chicago, IL 60605-2496
312/922-9410

Human Body Connection
Boston Museum of Science
Science Park
Boston, MA 02114
617/723-2500

Explore all the books in this series:

Animal Cells: Smallest Units of Life
ISBN: 0-7565-1616-1

Chemical Change: From Fireworks to Rust
ISBN: 0-7565-1256-5

DNA: The Master Molecule of Life
ISBN: 0-7565-1618-8

Erosion: How Land Forms, How It Changes
ISBN: 0-7565-0854-1

Genetics: A Living Blueprint
ISBN: 0-7565-1618-8

Manipulating Light: Reflection, Refraction, and Absorption
ISBN: 0-7565-1258-1

Minerals: From Apatite to Zinc
ISBN: 0-7565-0855-X

Natural Resources: Using and Protecting Earth's Supplies
ISBN: 0-7565-0856-8

Physical Change: Reshaping Matter
ISBN: 0-7565-1257-3

Plant Cells: The Building Blocks of Plants
ISBN: 0-7565-1619-6

Soil: Digging Into Earth's Vital Resources
ISBN: 0-7565-0857-6

Waves: Energy on the Move
ISBN: 0-7565-1259-X